CLIMBING THE PYRAMID

CLIMBING THE PYRAMID

The How-To's of Leadership

Michael B. Colegrove, Ph.D.

iUniverse, Inc.
New York Lincoln Shanghai

Climbing the Pyramid
The How-To's of Leadership

iUniverse, Inc.

For information address:
iUniverse, Inc.
2021 Pine Lake Road, Suite 100
Lincoln, NE 68512
www.iuniverse.com

ISBN: 0-595-31042-7

Printed in the United States of America

To Donna, whose love means the entire world to me.
You are my best friend, and I love you.

Contents

▼

Preface

We have all heard and probably used the phrase "climbing the ladder of success." I like to think that becoming a successful leader is more like climbing a pyramid. When we climb a ladder, the route is very narrowly defined. We can only see those above us and below us. Our primary focus must be the path ahead.

When climbing a pyramid, the route is less clearly defined. The side we are climbing is wide, with room to pass others and be passed. We can only see only one side of the pyramid, while the remaining three sides are not visible to us. For this reason, we do not have a clear picture as to how progress is being made on the sides we cannot view. Climbing a pyramid is harder and the footing is less sure.

This analogy illustrates the difficulty of rising to the top in the area of leadership. It shows how there is room to take alternate routes and how it is more difficult to monitor the progress of others. This example also shows us how easily we can be passed by an unseen competitor. We will never know our actual progress until we reach the peak and it may surprise us to find that others have reached the peak ahead of us.

The base of a pyramid is broad and secure. As we climb, the journey becomes less sure and more dangerous. For this reason, it is important for leaders to be well grounded in the fundamentals. At the base of the pyramid, leadership involves learning these fundamentals. When considering leadership, there are many factors that contribute to success; however, there is no substitute for a good beginning.

This book is a guide for those beginning the journey up the leadership pyramid as well as a reference for those already on the journey. It is my hope that this small book will become a tool to help leaders successfully negotiate the incline.

Mike Colegrove

Acknowledgments

I could not possibly list all the people who have been a positive influence in shaping my philosophy of leadership, but I would like to thank certain special people for their support, love, and prayers. To my wife and best friend, Donna, our daughter, Kimberly, and her husband, Matt. Also, to my colleagues, past and present, at Cumberland College and all the soldiers I have served with in the United States Army Reserve. A special thanks goes to my colleagues in the Department of Distance Education at the United States Army War College. During my service with them, I was guided to think strategically. Above all, I give thanks to my Heavenly Father for His inspiration, daily guidance, and wisdom.

THE PYRAMID: AN INTRODUCTION

Simply put, leadership is what gets things done in organizations, but there is much more to it than that. The nature of leadership is different as one progresses through an organization. The Leadership Pyramid below helps us understand the different leadership skills required at different levels.

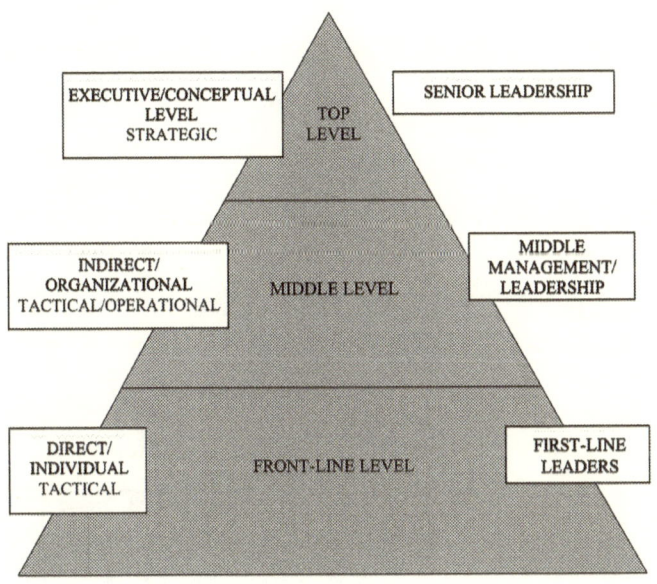

At the base of the pyramid, leadership is individual, or direct. By this we mean leading individuals or small groups in a direct, face-to-face manner. First-line leaders primarily lead in this way. In a sense, this is where training to become a more effective and responsible leader begins.

As a leader's responsibilities increase and she progresses to the middle of the pyramid, her skills must expand. Leaders at this level (and higher ones) must lead indirectly, through other leaders. In a sense, the individual becomes a leader of leaders. A middle manager cannot have the same type of direct influence on individual followers that first-line leadership offers.

At the highest level of the pyramid, senior leaders have additional and ever-increasing responsibilities. These leaders aim the organization in the right direction by establishing goals and priorities. These leaders must create a vision of what they want the organization to be. The ability to create an effective vision may be the greatest contribution of the senior leader. This requires strategic thinking.

This book focuses on the skills required to begin the journey in leadership development. These skills, used effectively by the new leader, will enable him or her to build a solid foundation and progress up the leadership pyramid. There is no substitute for a good beginning.

How to Plan

Setting a goal is not the main thing.
It is deciding how you will go
about achieving and staying with that plan.

—Tom Landry

Leaders at all levels need to plan for the future. The Estimate of the Situation is a good thinking tool with which you can start the process. In the military, the commander's estimate of the situation is a logical thinking process. Clearly defined, it is the process of reasoning by which a commander considers all circumstances affecting the situation and then chooses a course of action to accomplish the mission.

(See Appendix A—The Commander's Estimate of the Situation)

Applying this concept to civilian leadership is appropriate. A leader in any organization must give attention to detail; thus, the leader's estimate involves an analysis of an actual or contemplated operation in relation to the situation in which it will be conducted. This allows the leader to identify and appraise such factors as needed assets, potential obstacles, and consequences.

The leader's estimate requires clear thinking and attention to detail. It is at the heart of good planning.

When to Plan

- When you have been given a task or know that you have something to do.

How to Plan

- Determine whether you should develop the plan by yourself or get some subordinates involved.
  - Does time permit you to involve others?
  - Do others have the necessary skills and knowledge to assist you?
- List alternatives that you think might help you accomplish the task.
- Figure out the essential steps for each alternative.
- Put the steps in proper order.
- Determine when each step has to be finished.
- Pay close attention to any of the steps that your experience tells you could go wrong., and assume they will go wrong.
- For each alternative way of accomplishing the task, develop a plan that covers things that could go wrong.

How to Know When Planning Has Been Effective

- There are fewer "last-minute" problems.
- You can adjust quickly to changes and errors without getting rattled.

This analysis will benefit first-line leaders and middle managers. The process at the senior level involves a much more strategic approach. Long-range vision is required to steer the organization in the right direction. Strategic-planning skills become more valuable as one progresses further up the pyramid.

(See Appendix B—The Strategic Planning Model.)

How to Listen

A good listener tries to understand thoroughly
what the other person is saying. In the
end, he may disagree sharply; but before
he disagrees, he wants to know exactly what it is…

—Kenneth A. Wells

Effective communication is difficult, even under the best of circumstances. Leaders sometimes assume that communication is a 50/50 proposition. In reality, communication requires a 100% effort from each participant. This is almost impossible to accomplish, and as a result, many leadership efforts fail due to ineffective communication. The best a leader can do is commit himself to becoming an active partner in the communication processes. He can begin by becoming a good listener.

The most effective kind of listening is "active listening." When followers are listened to carefully, they will speak more carefully and will try to make clear exactly what they are feeling and thinking. The best way to get someone to listen carefully is to set the example: listen carefully to them. A revealing exercise is to test listening skills.

(See Appendix C—Listening Test)

When to Listen

- Whenever someone else is talking to you.

How to Listen

- Listen for total meaning—both the content of the message and any emotion associated with the message (e.g., anger, fear, happiness).

- Listen for both what a person says and how he says it. If it looks as though someone is so emotional that he is having trouble communicating with you, tell him about it (e.g., "Calm down, you aren't making sense").

- Test your understanding of the message. For example, while you're listening, ask, "May I repeat or restate what you've just said?"

- Listen to yourself while you're listening. If you're getting angry or excited inside, chances are, you're not listening as closely as you can be.

- Focus on the person communicating. Follow and understand the speaker as if you were walking in their shoes. Listen with your ears, but also with your eyes and other senses.

- Be aware: non-verbally acknowledge points in the speech. Let the argument or presentation run its course. Don't agree or disagree, but encourage the train of thought to develop.

- Be involved: Actively respond to questions and directions. Use body positioning (e.g., lean forward) and pay attention to encourage the speaker and signal your interest.

How to Know When You've Listened Well

- You begin to see your followers listening to you more carefully.

- In situations where you have to pass on information, you don't overlook things.

- More followers want to talk with you.

Active, effective listening is a habit, as well as, the foundation of effective communication.

(See Appendix D—*Jump Starting Your Listening Skills* by Dr. Tony Alessandra.)

How to Communicate

It is insight into human nature that is the key to the
communicator's skill. For whereas the writer is concerned
with what he puts into his writing, the communicator is
concerned with what the reader gets out of it.

—William Bernbach

Effective communication is an absolute must if we are to accomplish our mission. Leadership equals Communication, because leaders spend about 80 percent of their time communicating in some way. The leader, as she guides others in accomplishing a mission, has only one real tool: information. She does not handle followers; she motivates and organizes them to do their own work. Her primary tool to do all of this is the spoken or written word.

When to Communicate

- Whenever you must send a message to someone, spoken or written.

How to Communicate

- Make the message as simple as possible. Start with a clear, simple statement of purpose. Don't overload the message with unnecessary information.

- Organize the message in a way that is easily understood by the receiver. One of the keys to this is knowing your people.

- State the message in everyday language. Avoid jargon and overly complex words.

- Use examples to illustrate any major new points or ideas.

- Draw pictures and sketches to go along with words whenever possible. Use a blackboard, a notebook, or a stick in the sand.

- Repeat the important points at least twice.

- Summarize the major points of a message.

- Ask the receiver for feedback.

- When time permits, ask the receiver to repeat back or explain to you, in her own words, what you have just told her.

How to Know When You've Communicated Effectively

- The receiver gives you feedback that indicates she has understood the message.

- The receiver behaves in accordance with the intent of the message and you see her do what you had in mind.

(See Appendix E—Communication Skills Self-Assessment).

How to Manage Time

Don't say you don't have enough time.
You have exactly the same number of hours per day that was
given to Helen Keller, Pasteur, Michelangelo, Mother Teresa,
Leonardo da Vinci, Thomas Jefferson, and Albert Einstein.

—H. Jackson Brown

Time is the most precious human resource. Once used, time can never be recovered. The most important decisions made by leaders involve the use of time: what the leader will be doing with his time and what the followers will be doing with their time. One must not treat a resource as critical as time in a haphazard or careless manner. The use of time must be carefully planned and managed.

When to Manage Time

- When you notice you and your followers are not getting tasks done on time according to your own expectations or the schedules you're supposed to meet.

- When you end up scheduled to do two or more things at the same time.

- When you seem to forget about performing certain tasks until you are reminded, usually at the last minute.

- When your subordinates are complaining because things just don't seem organized.

How to Manage Time

- Buy or draw up a monthly calendar that gives you room to record scheduled activities on a daily basis.

- Keep the calendar up to date at all times. When you learn about an important activity, record it as soon as you can on your calendar.

- Start a "things to do" notebook. Each time you are told to perform a task or otherwise identify a task that must be performed, record the task and when it must be completed in this notebook. After you complete a task, cross out the entry in you notebook and record the time and date the task was completed.

- Establish time limits for meetings whenever possible. Record the main items discussed, make assignments, and set deadlines. (See Appendix F—Take Action Form for staff meetings).

- When a conflict arises regarding the use of time, establish your priorities based on your missions.

- Use the "1/3-2/3" rule. This rule allows the leader 1/3 of the available time leaving 2/3 available to subordinates.

- At least once a day, review your monthly calendar and your list of things to do. This should normally be done in the morning. When you have a lot to do in a day, write out a list of "things to do today" and list them in order of their priority. Do them in that order.

- Be prepared and be willing to work the amount of time needed to accomplish your mission. Don't plan your activities around an eight-hour day. Plan your day around your work activities.

A simple planning tool is an index card printed on both sides, as shown below:

Things to Do	Appointments	Date
	6:00	
	6:30	
	7:00	
	7:30	
	8:00	
	8:30	
	9:00	
	9:30	
	10:00	
	10:30	
	11:00	
	11:30	
	12:00	
	12:30	
	1:00	
	1:30	
	2:00	
	2:30	
	3:00	
	3:30	
	4:00	
	4:30	
	5:00	
	5:30	
	6:00	
	6:30	
	7:00	
	7:30	
	8:00	
	8:30	
	9:00	
	9:30	
	10:00	

How to Know When You've Managed Time Effectively

- All required tasks seem to be accomplished on time.

- Conflicts in your schedule don't occur.

- Things seem to run "smoothly."

- Followers aren't surprised when you ask them about tasks they are supposed to have done.

How to Set
Expectations

High expectations
are the key to everything.

—Sam Walton

"You often get what you expect." As a leader, you must harness this very powerful reality to work for you. It is your job to set and use expectations in a manner that supports and enhances performance.

The theory that expectations affect performance is known as the Pygmalion Principle. Its name is derived from a Greek myth in which a sculptor named Pygmalion sculpted a statue of a woman and fell in love with it. His love was so strong that it transformed the statue into a real woman. Research in the field of education has supported the theory by demonstrating that students who the teacher believed were smarter than the rest of the group (when they were actually randomly chosen) performed substantially better than those believed to be "average." In these experiments, the only difference between the students who performed best and the rest of the group was the teacher's expectations. As a leader, you also have the power to influence follower performance through your expectations.

A second theory that is relevant to this topic is the Expectancy Theory. The Expectancy Theory states that followers are motivated to perform by an expected reward and that the level of performance can be determined by the attractiveness of the reward. Therefore, it can be concluded that determining potential rewards and conveying them to followers is an important part of setting expectations.

A leader can use work planning to set effective expectations. Work planning is a process whereby the leader and the followers discuss expectations. The leader normally either asks the follower what she can accomplish or tells her what the expectations are. They can then discuss how realistic these expectations are, plan how to meet them, and discuss what rewards will be given for successfully completing each step of the process. This involves setting plans on the following levels: plans for the overall job, annual plans, quarterly plans, weekly plans, and daily plans. Once plans are set, you must maintain good communication and follow up on how well the plans are carried out and whether revision is needed. This is effective because followers get lots of feedback, and you will not be surprised if something does not turn out as originally planned. You are able to proactively handle any potential problems and consistently convey the high level of expectations you have for your subordinates.

The best way to make sure that jobs and tasks are done right is to see to it that clear, precise expectations are set. People work best when they know exactly what is expected of them. The most effective expectations are those that are realistic, challenging, specific, measurable, and doable with a specific timeframe. In assigning tasks, leaders should never assume that followers are already aware of the expectations upon them.

When to Set Expectations

- When your followers appear willing and are trying, but their performance doesn't meet the required level for mission accomplishment.

- When you have a new task to get done and the expectations are unclear or have not yet been established.

- When followers ask a lot of questions or seem confused about expected outcomes.

How to Set Expectations

- When expectations aren't specified, determine what they should be.

- Communicate expectations to your followers.

- Show examples of desired expectations if you can.

- Check to see if the expectations are understood.

- Measure performance against the stated expectations rather than against others' performances.

- When individuals are not able to meet expectations, right away they should be led step-by-step to the desired standard.

- When you have specified expectations, always provide feedback as to how well expectations are being met.

- Reevaluate expectations when they appear inappropriate (too easy, too hard).

How to Know When You've Set the Right Expectations

- There are very few questions and little confusion during the course of accomplishing a task.

- Followers are self-confident and proud of their work.

- Followers appear to be dissatisfied with poor or sloppy work.

How to Inspect

What is best done
is most inspected.

—Anonymous

Inspections can have a powerful positive effect on individuals and organizations. They can also have a powerful negative effect. When followers have worked hard to get ready for inspection, leaders must be ready to inspect.

When to Inspect

- When you want to ensure uniform compliance with established expectations and proper operating procedures.

- When you want to check current status. (This is the primary purpose of making unannounced inspections. Unannounced inspections also save preparatory time.)

- When the situation seems to require a thorough, detailed check. A critical event or test may need a complete, top-to-bottom inspection.

How to Inspect

- Prepare for the inspection. At the first-line level, this means having the appropriate knowledge.

- Learn the established expectations and requirements.

- Have a plan for inspecting. Rehearse what you're going to do.

- Inform your followers (well ahead of time) of the details of what is to be inspected, where the inspection will be held, when it will occur, who will inspect, and why the inspection is being done.

- Conduct the inspection. Keep it formal and businesslike.

- Pay attention to detail.

- Check what you see against established expectations.

- Record deficiencies and note the responsible individuals or teams.

- Check that items are serviceable and note needed repairs. Don't just casually look.

- Check to see that the inspected equipment works. To do this, you have to know how to "work" the equipment yourself.

- Analyze the results. For example, check results against previous inspections to see whether things are getting better or worse.

- Plan corrective action: who, what, and when.

- Communicate inspection results to subordinates. Provide a detailed critique. Feedback to subordinates can be a powerful leadership tool if given in the proper way.

- Re-inspect if you're not satisfied with the results. If you're not satisfied with what you've seen and you do not re-inspect, then no matter what you say, you have automatically lowered the expectations. Never hesitate to re-inspect.

How to Know When Inspections Have Been Conducted Properly

- Individual and organizational equipment is on hand and being properly maintained.

- You see uniformity of appearance and performance.

- Established policies and procedures are being followed and established expectations are being met.

How to Provide Corrective Feedback

The majority of people have not the courage to correct others because they don't have the courage to bear correction themselves.

—Source Unknown

Leaders must give their followers feedback in order to help them learn their jobs and overcome substandard performances. Frequently when discussing job-related problems with a subordinate, a leader may put the follower on the defensive. Typical defensive reactions will include the following: denying any wrongdoing, blaming someone else, reacting aggressively, offering excuses, and reacting emotionally. The best way for a leader to avoid this is to focus her feedback on the task and on what the follower did, not on the traits of the follower herself.

When to Give Feedback

- Whenever a follower's performance fails to meet a standard

How to Give Feedback

McGill and Beatty (in *Action Learning: A Practitioner's Guide*, London: Kogan, 1994) provide useful suggestions about giving effective feedback:

- Clarity—Be clear about what you want to say.
- Emphasize the positive—This isn't being collusive in the person's dilemma.

- Be specific—Avoid general comments and clarify pronouns such as "it," "that," etc.

- Focus on behavior rather than the person.

- Refer to behavior that can be changed.

- Be descriptive rather than evaluative.

- Own the feedback—Use 'I' statements.

- Generalizations—Notice "all," "never," "always," etc., and ask to get specificity. Often these words place arbitrary limits on behavior.

- Be very careful with advice—People rarely struggle with an issue because of the lack of some specific piece of information; often, the best we can do is help the person come to a better understanding of their issue, how it developed, and how they can identify actions to address the problem more effectively.

How to Know When You've Given the Right Feedback

- The follower can tell you exactly what you have judged as poor, she can tell you why it is poor, and she can tell you what she is going to do about it.

How to Reward

Ask someone else how he knows when he has done a good job. For some people, the proof comes from the outside. The boss pats you on the back and says your work was great. You get a raise. You win a big award. Your work is noticed and applauded by your peers.

—Tony Robbins

Rewards are the most powerful tools available to leaders in creating a motivating environment. A reward shows right while punishment shows wrong. Sometimes, a leader wants a follower to know what's wrong, but most often a leader wants the follower to know what's right. In terms of getting the mission accomplished, reward is more effective and takes less time to administer than punishment. In addition, rewards help increase the confidence and trust between follower and leader. Confidence and trust are necessary for success.

When to Reward

- When a follower has met or exceeded a standard for performance. Some leaders will tell you they reward only their best followers. That's not the way to reward. It's fine to recognize the best workers occasionally, but make sure that you are also rewarding the others who have met your expectations. The objective is to develop a team where all members meet performance expectations. Everyone can be good, but everyone can't be the best. Show the good individuals that you value their performance, too.

How to Reward

- Make sure that the individual is due a reward, that his performance has met or exceeded the performance standard.

- If you have promised an individual a specific reward, give it to her. Don't make promises or hint about rewards unless you know you can deliver. Make sure the reward means something to the individual.

- Remember that rewards take many forms: a "Good work!" a "Thank You," a pat on the back, an afternoon off, recognition in front of peers, positive written evaluations, etc. Use them all. Fit the reward to the performance.

- Follow through. Make sure that your followers get the rewards they deserve. Whenever possible, do the rewarding in front of others, especially members of the same team.

- Give new team members extra attention as far as rewarding goes. Because they are new, almost any reward will have extra value.

How to Know When You've Used Rewards Effectively

- Followers' performance continues to meet or exceed the established expectations.

- Followers' morale is improved.

How to Punish

He who does not punish evil
commands it to be done.

—Leonardo da Vinci

Punishment should be the used as a last resort to improve performance. There are several reasons for this. Punishment doesn't teach a follower what he should do. Instead, it teaches him that he should avoid getting caught when he doesn't do what should be done. Punishment might also lead to hate, which makes it pretty difficult to build trust, respect, and a sense of teamwork between a follower and his leader. Finally, repeated punishment tells a man he's a "loser." This means extra work for you if you're trying to develop individuals who have confidence in their ability to win. However, don't let anyone tell you that punishment should never be used. It has its place, it works, and it should be used when necessary to improve performance.

When to Punish

- Punish an individual for poor performance when all of the following conditions have been met:
  - The follower has failed to meet a performance standard of which he was aware.
  - You are convinced he is unwilling and doesn't appear to be trying to perform the assigned task.
  - The follower has been warned that he will be punished if he fails to perform to the standard.

How to Punish

- Apply punishment as quickly as possible after the poor performance. Make sure the follower fully understands that the punishment is a direct result of a specific failure to meet expectations.

- Guidelines for punishment from Ormrod, *Human Learning*, 3rd ed. (City of Publication: Prentice Hall, 1998):

  - Be sure it is really punishing.

  - Be strong but not severe

  - Threaten first, but carry through.

  - Describe clearly the behavior being punished.

  - Apply punishment consistently.

  - Change the environment to stop the behavior.

  - Teach better behavior.

  - Punish immediately.

  - Avoid some punishment depending on the person.

  - Use punishment sparingly.

How to Know When Punishment Has Been Applied Correctly

- The follower's behavior and performance improve.

How to Counsel

You cannot teach a man anything; you can
only help him find it within himself.

—Galileo

Effective counseling helps the individual understand what his problems are then helps him get started solving those problems. The leader's goal in counseling is to make followers more effective on the job. The objective of all counseling sessions is to help the individual solve his own problems. Counseling is a complex skill and is an important part of a leader's duties.

When to Counsel

- When the follower's attitude or actions have changed markedly and you think he may be having problems that require help in solving.

- When a subordinate leader brings a follower to you for counseling.

- When a follower asks you for help or advice.

How to Counsel

- Make yourself available. Don't just schedule open-door time or tell your followers, "Come see me if you have any problems." Get out and make yourself available.

- Don't ignore or joke about people with problems. Try to build the reputation you deal with your followers' problems honestly, fairly, and effectively.

- Listen. Stay quiet and let the follower do the talking.

- Take your time and be patient.

- Get the follower to state his problem specifically. Ask him, "Can you tell me more?" Tell him, "I don't understand what you mean by so and so" or "Would you give me an example of that?"

- If you think that something can be done about the problem, work with the follower to reach an agreement on what he should do to solve it.

- Keep on the subject.

- Make sure the conversation focuses on what the follower wants to talk about. Your own war stories usually don't help very much.

- Gather as much information as possible about the problem.

- Have the individual explain points in greater detail if necessary.

- Don't get mad or argumentative about what he says. Keep on listening. Let him talk.

- At this point, think about all you've heard and determine whether the individual needs help. You should send him for special help only if—

  - the problem is too difficult for you.

  - there is a language or cultural barrier.

  - you think you are not making any progress.

  - you think you are too personally involved in the problem.

  - he obviously needs expert knowledge that you don't have.

- If you send him to someone else, make the appointment for him.

- Check to make sure he has kept the appointment.

- Talk to him after his appointment to make sure he believes he's getting the help he needs.

- Follow up on the counseling session:

- Make sure he does everything he told you he would do to solve his problem.

- Have him establish intermediate goals if necessary.

- Check on his progress from time to time. Each time, get him to talk. You listen.

- Document the counseling session.

(See Appendix G—Record of Counseling Form)

How to Know When You've Given Good Counsel

- The follower tells you that the problem is solved.

- The attitude or actions that first led you to suspect that there was a problem start changing for the better.

- The individual returns to work and there is a change in his attitude and actions.

How to Motivate

Motivation is the practice of creating an environment in which followers move themselves toward positive performance.

—Michael B. Colegrove

Motivation does not require an elaborate definition. Motivation is simply a set of needs and desires; it is the underlying basis for what individuals think and do. Individuals act in their own best interest. Followers work hardest when they are working toward group goals that also satisfy their own needs. To motivate effectively, leaders need to recognize that individuals are complex and variable, that they change their behavior over time (not overnight), that they need variety in their work, that they want to do worthwhile things, and that they respond differently to leadership practices. Knowing your people takes a lot of listening, watching, and thinking. Do these things well, and you can create a motivating environment for your followers.

When to Motivate

- Constantly.

How to Motivate

- Always pay close attention to basic physical needs—food, shelter, clothing, etc.

- Talk with your followers and listen to them.

- Identify the things that are important to them—their needs.

- Evaluate how accomplishing the mission will satisfy these needs. Explain this to subordinates.

- Set the example in everything you do.

- Reward only those who earn it.

- Punish all of those who deserve it.

- Explain how important each individual's competence is to the job.

How to Know When You've Motivated Well

- A follower's behavior changes in the desired direction.

How to Ask the Right Questions

One who asks a question is a fool for five minutes; one who does not ask a question remains a fool forever.

—Chinese proverb

Lead by asking, not by telling. As a leader, the material you work with is people, and most of the problems you have to solve are people problems. You can't solve any of these problems without information, and the information you need to solve them can only be found in the people themselves. To get it, you can't rely on paper alone. Reports, records, charts, and numbers will help a little, but to get the information you need to solve problems, you have to talk with people. And when you do that, you have to know how to ask questions.

When to Ask Questions

- Ask questions any time you need additional information or clarification.

How to Ask Questions

Here are six guidelines on developing the critical leadership skill of asking questions:

1.   Don't ask questions that can be answered with a simple "yes" or "no." Instead, ask leading questions that require in-depth explanations, then listen carefully as the follower explains, trying to "read between the lines" as you do so.

2. Don't ask questions that would require him to be outwardly critical of his organization or chain of command. The vast majority of people don't want to get their leaders into trouble, even if they feel it would be justified. In other words, don't put the follower on the spot.

3. Steer clear of vague, general questions that will invariably illicit vague, general answers. Such questions serve to make conversation, but not communication.

4. Learn how to tactfully, indirectly, quietly, and politely challenge the automatic answers. Short, meaningless answers provide no useful information.

5. Work constantly to get the individual to elaborate on his answers. Get into the habit of probing: "Why do you think this is so?" "When did you last do such and such?" "Where did you learn that?" "Who taught it to you?" "How would you do this or that?" "What do you think of this policy or that requirement?" As a general rule, every other question should start with a why when, where, who, how, or what.

6. Be a leader, not a lawyer. Before asking a hard question that the follower might hesitate to answer, set him at ease. Don't try to pressure, trick, or trap him.

How to Know When You've Asked the Right Questions

- You have all the information you need to address a situation.

How to Use Power

We thought, because we had power, we had wisdom.

—Stephen Vincent Bennet, *Litany for Dictatorships*

Power is the potential for one person to influence the behavior of others. In this chapter we will consider outcomes of power, influence processes, types of power, and types of influence behavior.

All leaders have power. Early on in our development as leaders we must decide how to use this power, and there are a number of old myths that may hinder us.

The first myth is that power is evil and corrupting, and that it is always used by the few power holders to block change that could benefit others. We might even believe that good people should avoid power. However, the reality is that we cannot realize our values or goals without power. Power enables us to forge relationships with others and to bring about positive change.

The second myth relates to the availability of power. Since there is only so much of it to go around, the more power someone else has, the less there is for me. The reality is that power comes from the relationships we build with others. The more we use our power, the more power there is to use.

The third myth is that power is a one-way force, that when one is in control, he or she can get others to do exactly what they want. However, we must understand that power always exists in relationships. The actions of each individual affect the other, so no one is ever completely powerless.

Outcomes of Power

The leader's attempt to influence the follower can result in the following three qualitatively distinct outcomes:

1. Commitment. This describes an outcome in which the follower whole-heartedly agrees with a decision or request from the leader and does his best to carry out the request or implement the decision.

2. Compliance. This describes an outcome in which the follower is willing to do what the leader asks but is apathetic rather than enthusiastic about it and makes only a minimal effort to carry out the request.

3. Resistance. This describes an outcome in which the follower is opposed to the proposal or request, rather than merely indifferent about it, and actively attempts to avoid carrying it out.

Influence Processes

The leader may influence the follower through the following three qualitatively distinct processes, which may occur at the same time or independently:

1. Instrumental Compliance. The follower carries out a request for the purpose of obtaining a tangible reward or avoiding punishment. Compliance is likely to result.

2. Internalization. The follower commits his support and implements the leader's proposal because it is intrinsically desirable and adheres to his values. Commitment is likely to result.

3. Personal Identification. The follower imitates the leader's behavior or adopts the same attitudes to please the leader and to emulate the leader. The follower is motivated by the need for acceptance.

Types of Power

Researchers French and Raven have developed the following taxonomy of power. They have identified five different types and classified them according to their source:

1. Reward Power. The follower complies in order to obtain rewards controlled by the leader. Reward power tends to be most effective when the leader

    *   Offers the type of rewards that people want

    *   Offers rewards that are fair and ethical

    *   Doesn't promise more than he can deliver

    *   Explains the criteria for giving rewards and keeps them simple

    *   Provides rewards as promised if requirements are met

    *   Uses rewards symbolically to recognize accomplishments

2. Coercive Power. The follower complies in order to avoid punishment. Coercive power tends to be most effective when the leader

    *   Explains the rules and requirements so that the follower understands the consequences

    *   Responds promptly and consistently without showing favoritism

    *   Expresses a sincere desire to help the follower to comply

    *   Invites the person to suggest ways to correct the problem

    *   Uses punishments that are legitimate

3. Legitimate Power. The follower complies because he believes that the leader has the right to make the request and that he is obliged to comply. This kind of power tends to stem from formal authority. Legitimate power is most effective when the leader

    *   Makes polite, clear requests

    *   Explains the reasons for the requests

    *   Doesn't exceed her scope of authority

    *   Follows up to verify compliance

4. Expert Power. The follower complies because he or she believes that the leader has specific knowledge about the best way to do something. Expert power tends to be most effective when the leader

    *   Explains the reasons for making a request

- Provides evidence for why a proposal will be successful

- Doesn't exaggerate or misrepresent facts

- Listens carefully to the follower's concerns and suggestions

- Acts confidently and decisively

5. Referent Power. The follower complies because he or she identifies with or admires the leader and wants to gain the leader's approval. Referent power tends to be most effective when the leader

- Shows acceptance and positive regard

- Acts supportive and helpful

- Performs unsolicited favors

- Makes self-sacrifices to show concern

- Keeps promises

French, John R.P. and Bertram Raven. "Bases of Social Power." <u>Studies in Social Power</u>. Ed. Dorwin Cartwright. University of Michigan, Ann Arbor,1959.

Types of Influence Behavior

Researchers have recently begun to examine the specific types of behavior used to exercise influence, rather than focusing only on power. The following are the eleven most commonly identified influence tactics:

1. Rational Persuasion. The leader uses rational arguments and factual evidence to show a proposal or request is feasible and relevant in completing important objectives. This tactic tends to be used to make an initial request and has proven highly effective.

2. Apprising. The leader explains how carrying out a request or supporting a proposal will benefit the follower personally or help advance the follower's career. This tactic tends to be moderately effective.

3. Inspirational appeals. The leader makes an appeal to values and ideals or seeks to arouse the follower's emotions to gain commitment. This tactic tends to be used in combination with other tactics and has proven highly effective.

4.   Consultation. The leader encourages the follower to suggest improve-
     ments in a proposal or to help plan an activity for which the follower's
     support and assistance are desired. This tactic tends to be used in combi-
     nation with other tactics and has proven highly effective.

5.   Exchange. The leader offers an incentive, suggests an exchange of favors,
     or indicates willingness to reciprocate at a later time if the follower does
     what the leader requests. This tactic has proven moderately effective.

6.   Collaboration. The leader offers to provide relevant resources and assis-
     tance if the follower carries out a request. This tactic tends to be used for
     immediate follow-up and has proven highly effective.

7.   Personal appeals. The leader asks the follower to carry out a request or
     support a proposal out of friendship, or she asks for a personal favor
     before saying what it is. This tactic tends to be used more for an initial
     request and has proven moderately effective.

8.   Ingratiation. The leader uses praise and flattery before or during an
     influence attempt or expresses confidence in the follower's ability to
     carry out a difficult request. This tactic tends to be used more for an ini-
     tial request and has proven moderately effective.

9.   Legitimating tactics. The leader seeks to establish the legitimacy of a
     request by referring to rules, formal policies, or official documents. This
     tactic tends to be used for immediate follow-up and has not proven to
     be very effective.

10. Pressure. The leader uses demands, threats, frequent checkups, or persis-
     tent reminders to influence the follower. This tactic tends to be used for
     delayed follow-up and has not proven to be very effective.

11. Coalition tactics. The leader seeks the aid of others to persuade the fol-
     lower to do something or uses the support of others as a reason for the
     follower to agree. This tactic tends to be used for delayed follow-up and
     has not proven to be very effective.

—Yukl, G., *Leadership in Organizations* (Upper Saddle River, NJ: Prentice Hall,
2002).

Deciding how to use power is a challenge for the leader. The following Chinese
proverb gives useful advice on the matter:

Water is fluid, soft and yielding.
But water will wear away rock, which is rigid and cannot yield.
As a rule, whatever is fluid, soft, and yielding will overcome
whatever is rigid and hard.

The wise leader knows that yielding overcomes resistance, and gentleness melts rigid defenses. A wise leader does not fight the force of the group's energy but flows and yields and absorbs and lets go.

What is soft is strong.

How to Develop Vision

Where there is no vision the
people perish.

—Proverbs 29: 18

In his book *Visionary Leadership*, Bert Nanus says, "Effective leaders adopt challenging new visions of what is possible and desirable, communicate their vision, and persuade others to become so committed to these new directions that they are eager to lend their resources and energy to make them happen." Leaders are there to coach, direct, and nudge followers in the direction of their goals. They are able to pass their intensity along to their followers.

A leader guides followers without ruling them. He charts a course, gives direction, and develops the social and psychological environment. The leader provides an atmosphere where others can learn and grow. He must give some responsibility to the group and encourage independence. This will empower followers and make them feel trusted. There must be a balance, where the leader accepts responsibility while empowering followers to act.

Excellence in leadership is acquired by people who have a strong sense of vision, have passion, and are able to get people to commit 100% to making their vision become a reality. Great leaders excel in the art of creating a motivating environment, fostering mutual respect, instilling confidence and enthusiasm, and showing credibility.

How to Develop Vision

Imagine your organization at a time in the future being "the best it can be." How would it look? Below are some areas of consideration:

- values

- goals

- achievements

- team contributions

- employee development

- talents that contributed to success

- recognition received

- obstacles overcome

- customer satisfaction

- revenue, market-share growth

- risks

- changes made

- flexibility to respond to change

- span of influence

- success

The next challenge is to shape your thoughts into a message or a few thoughtfully crafted statements that will help you share your vision of the future with others and enlist them in it.

Vision Statements

Vision statements articulate as clearly as possible why an organization exists and put into words the desired future state of an organization. A vision is a stated goal that provides direction, aligns key players, and energizes people to achieve a common purpose. It states your organizational ideal, stretching the imagination and motivating people to rethink what is possible. Developing a clear vision statement is the most critical element of a successful organization-wide transformation and is the essence of strategic planning.

Vision statements should represent your organization completely. They will clearly state your goals and ideals and concisely communicate these points to your followers.

What Are the Benefits?

A vision statement looks at the future with an optimistic yet realistic perspective. It communicates values, unifies people at all levels toward a common goal, empowers an enterprise, builds on the past, develops and communicates common values throughout the organization, increases commitment from leaders and followers, and brings focus and clarity to the future.

How to Know If Your Vision Statement Is Effective

- Followers buy into the vision and are eager to contribute to the process.

(See Appendix H—Creating an Organizational Vision)

Summary

Know your enemy and
know yourself and you can
fight a hundred battles without disaster.

—Sun Tzu

Leaders are in the business of personal and personnel development. It is necessary for us to know as much as we can about ourselves. We must know about others as well, but the journey begins with self-understanding.

(See Appendix H—*Motivational Management: Developing Leadership Skills,* by Diane M. Eade.)

Many aspiring leaders seek to find the source of their leadership potential. This is found in an honest understanding of strengths in relationship to the situation. If we understand our strengths and seek to develop them, we can increase our potential for success in the leadership arena.

The situation is constantly changing. Part of understanding oneself is being mindful of the situation for which we are preparing. The constant interplay between strengths and the situation results in a fluctuation of the potential to lead. This is best depicted by the figure below.

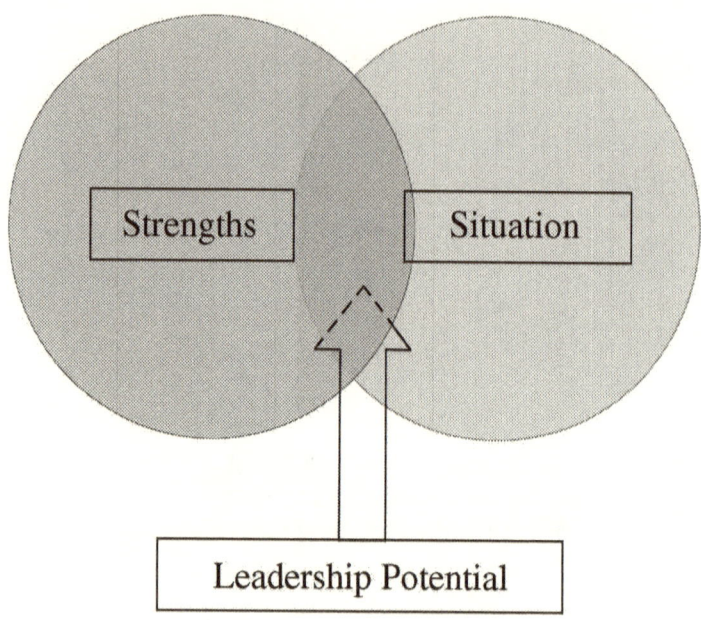

Leadership potential exists in the area where strengths and situation overlap. This increases or decreases in relation to the strength/situation match. When the leader understands his strengths and develops them with a future situation in mind, he is preparing for success. The leader must realize that he has control over both strengths and situation. The leadership-progression matrix below will help the developing leader know exactly what to look for at each level of the journey up the pyramid.

LEADERSHIP PROGRESSION

(CLIMBING THE PYRAMID)

FIRST-LINE LEADER	MIDDLE MANAGEMENT	SENIOR LEADER
Becomes acquainted with things	Controls things	Creates things
Supervises people and things	Keeps track of people and things	Changes things
Needs, requests, and uses resources	Budgets, makes ends meet	Finds resources
Acquires the basic knowledge to plan and does basic planning	Plans	Defines the mission
Sets Priorities	Organizes	Creates an environment
Identifies Problems	Solves problems	Shakes things up
Has face-to-face contact with customers and followers	Copes with complexity	Sets direction and tone

Works with staff	Staffs jobs and tasks, external locus of control	Aligns people, internal locus of control, creative risk taker
Gains an understanding of the rules and follows them	Promotes rule-orientation, system-based	Imagination-based
Interacts with outsiders and insiders	Interacts internally, keeps people in line with systems	Interacts with outsiders, inspires people
Responsible for team effort	Responsible for performance of organization	Responsible for overall outcome
Works with a team	Uses deductive process	Uses inductive process
Provides feedback to organization	Monitors organizational culture	Monitors outside culture
Sees the road ahead	Begins to enjoy the view	Is near or at the top

The information provided will allow for timely alterations in personal development and course corrections in your journey. By keeping a close check on progress and making good decisions along the way, the leader maximizes his or her potential.

A leader is able to control her choice of paths and the development of her strengths. The leader is in charge and can influence the strength and situation interaction If this concept is understood and aggressively implemented, the trip up the pyramid will be a positive and fulfilling adventure. Remember the following quote from General George Patton, Jr.:

"Accept the challenges so that you can feel the exhilaration of victory."

Appendix A
The Commander's Estimate of the Situation

The leader uses the command and control process to figure out what is going on, decide what to do about it, tell soldiers what to do, and then keep track of how well his soldiers are doing. The troop-leading procedures are the leader's tools to guide the command and control process. These procedures provide a common framework for all echelons of command to apply the command and control process. Two other tools that are part of this process are the estimate of the situation and METT-T (Mission, Enemy, Terrain, Troops and Time) analysis. The relationship of these three tools is depicted below

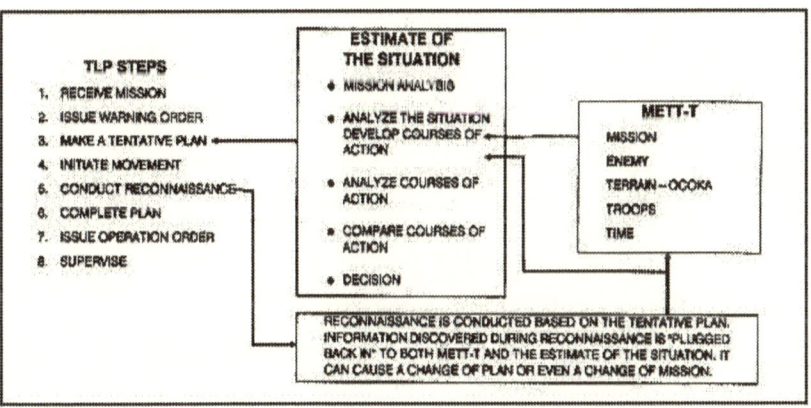

The estimate of the situation is the Army's decision-making process. It helps the leader determine his mission, understand his situation, and select the best course of action to accomplish his assigned responsibilities. Leaders use the estimate for every tactical decision. Their experience, ability, and the time available will determine the amount of detailed analysis in each estimate. The estimate is a continuous process; the commanding officer constantly receives information about the situation. Whenever he receives the information (during planning, en route to the objective, or just before the assault begins), he must decide if this information affects his mission. If it does, then he decides how to adjust his plan to meet this new situation. It is only through the estimate process, however hasty, that the leader can make the proper decision.

The estimate has five steps.

1. Conduct a detailed mission analysis.

2. Analyze the situation and develop courses of action.

3. Analyze courses of action (wargame).

4. Compare courses of action.

5. Make a decision.

Taken from FM 100-5. Operations. 5 May 1986

Appendix B
Strategic-Planning Model

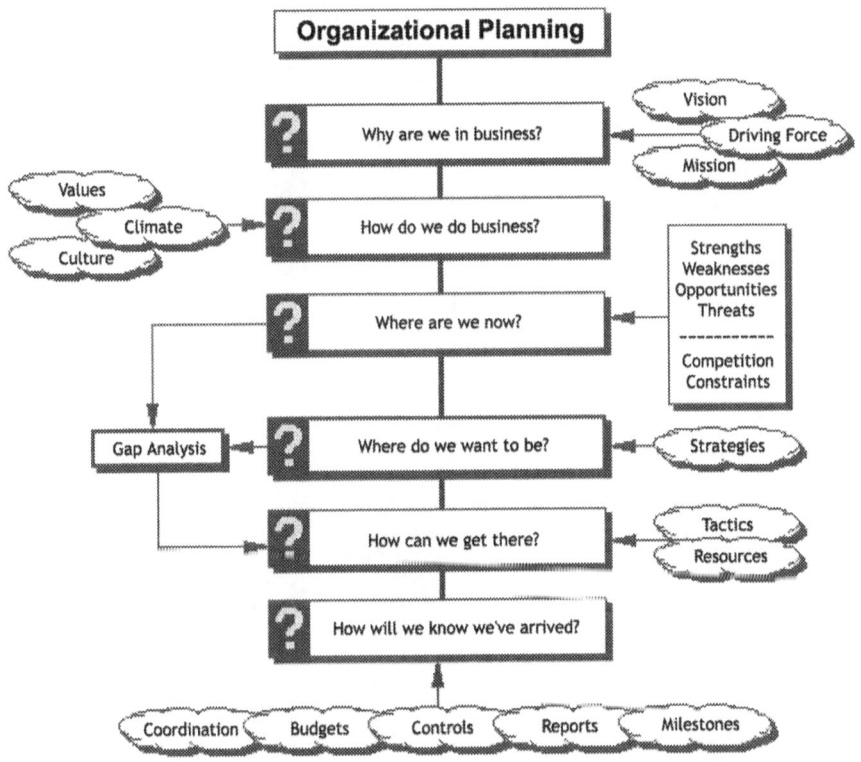

The most important parts of this model are the questions. These questions are appropriate in any strategic-planning situation.

Gap Analysis refers to the process of determining to what extent environmental factors might lead to gaps between what is being achieved and what could be achieved if changes in existing strategies are made.

Appendix C
Listening Test

In any job where work must be done with or through people, effective listening is crucial. For this warm-up, each participant needs a piece of paper and a pen or pencil.

Instructions:

Write #1 in the upper portion of the paper and answer this question:

1. In this list of names—George, John, David, Adam, James, Grace—which names begin with a J?

Underneath your answer, write the numbers 2a and 2b.

2. Suppose you were given these directions: "Go to Room 3-1-5 and look in the lower right-hand drawer and bring me all the boxes of pencils that are there."

    A.   Would you look in the right- or left-hand drawer?

    B.   Would you go to Room 5-3-1, 3-1-5, or 1-3-5?

Now write the number 3.

3. Answer true or false to this:

"In the list of words, BEE, SEE, FREE, GLEE, FLEA, ME, the second word is FREE."

Now write the number 4.

> 4. Your wife asks you to bring home meat, milk, cheese, and bread. You bring home milk, peas, bread, and meat. What did you forget?

Now write the number 5.

> 5. You are the driver of a school bus. At the first stop, thirteen children get on. At the next stop, five children get on and two get off. At the next stop eight children get on. At the next stop, four more get on and one sneaks off. How old is the bus driver?

Now check the answers and score the quiz:

1. 20 points if they wrote James and John.
2a. 10 points if they wrote right drawer.
2b. 10 points if they wrote 3-1-5.
3. 20 points if they wrote false.
4. 20 points if they wrote cheese.
5. 20 points if they wrote their own age.

100—Excellent Listener
90—Good Listener
80—Fair, Can Improve
70—Need Help!
60 or below—Wow!

Appendix D
Jump-Starting Your Listening Skills

by Dr. Tony Alessandra

Most of us have lots of room for improvement when it comes to listening. I encourage you to practice these ten tips to make active listening easier for you. Like anything new, they won't feel natural until you've used them a lot. But do so and you'll definitely be on your way to improving this aspect of your salesmanship. Remember this—whether you are selling an idea to your child or spouse, selling a solution in a customer-service session, selling a new way of doing things to your employees or co-workers, or selling a product or service to a customer— "People Don't Buy Because They're Made to Understand; They Buy Because They Feel Understood." This requires superior listening skills!

1. Listen—really listen—to one person for one day. Choose one person you could relate to better than you currently do. Commit to listening to them— not just hearing them—for one day. After each meeting, ask yourself: Did I use the CARESS techniques? Did I really make an effort to go beyond superficialities? Did I observe verbal, vocal, and visual clues? Did I note what was not being said as well as what was said? [See the author's note at the end of this article for an explanation of CARESS.]

    Once you've gotten into the habit of nudging yourself to listen better, extend this exercise to successive days and to other acquaintances. Listening well is a gift you can give to others. It'll cost you nothing, but it may be invaluable to them.

2. Create a receptive listening environment. Turn off the TV. Hold your calls. Put away your spreadsheets and silence your computer. When listening, forget about clipping your nails, crocheting, solving crossword puzzles, or snapping your chewing gum. Instead, try to provide a private, quiet, comfortable setting where you sit side by side with others without distractions. If that's not possible, perhaps suggest a later meeting in a more neutral, quieter environment.

    The point is to make your partner feel like you're there for him or her. Don't be like the boss who put a desk-sized model of a parking meter on his desk, then required employees to feed the meter—ten cents for every ten minutes of conversation. What a signal he was sending out!

3. Don't talk when I'm interrupting. If someone else is interrupting, avoid the temptation to reply in kind. It'll just raise the level of acrimony and widen the gulf between you. Instead, be the one who shows restraint by listening to them, then quietly, calmly, taking up where you left off.

    "If you're talking, you aren't learning," President Lyndon Johnson used to say. And by showing more courtesy than your adversary, you will be quietly sending a message as to how you both ought to be acting.

4. Don't overdo it. Sometimes newcomers to the skill of listening can get carried away. They know they're supposed to make eye contact, so they'll stare so much the speaker feels intimidated. Taught to nod their heads to show they're comprehending, they'll start bobbing like sailboats on a rough sea. Having learned to project appropriate facial expressions while listening, they'll look as if they're suffering from gastric distress.

    Eventually, the speaker will figure out that the other person has recently attended a "listening" seminar or read a book on the subject. But it all comes across as artificial. All good things, including listening, require moderation and suitable application. Too much exaggerated listening is just as bad as, if not worse than, none at all.

5. Practice mind-mapping. An excellent method for note-taking is "mind-mapping." This free-form technique helps you take notes quickly without breaking the flow of the conversation. Essentially, you use a rough diagram to

connect primary pieces of information, then break it into appropriate sub-topics or details.

It's extremely helpful and easy to use and not at all like the old-fashioned Roman-numeral kind of outlining you probably learned in school. If you want to know more, I recommend Tony Buzan's excellent *The Mind Map Book*.

6.   Be alert to your body language. What you do with your eyes, face, hands, arms, legs, and posture sends out signals as to whether you are, or aren't, listening to and understanding what the other person is saying. For example, if you noticed someone you were talking to doing the following, what would you think?

- Glancing sideways

- Sighing

- Yawning

- Frowning

- Crossing arms on chest

- Looking at the ceiling

- Cleaning fingernails

- Cracking knuckles

- Jingling change or rattling keys

- Fidgeting in chair

You'd very quickly get the impression—wouldn't you?—that no matter what that person was saying, he or she actually has zero interest in what you're talking about and wishes you'd just go away. As Ralph Waldo Emerson said, "What you are is shouting so loud, I can't hear what you are saying."

Conversely, consider these mannerisms:

- Looking into your eyes

- Smiling frequently

- Raising eyebrows periodically

- Grinning at appropriate moments

- Using expressive hand gestures when speaking

- Keeping eyes wide open

- Licking lips

- Tilting head

- Leaning toward you

This person shows interest in you and what you're saying. In addition, the active listener usually acknowledges the speaker verbally as well, with such comments as "I see," "Uh-huh," "Mmmm," or "Really?"

In a later chapter, you'll learn how some people are contact-oriented, while others are much less so, preferring more space between themselves and the people they're talking to. You'll be a better listener if you honor those spatial preferences.

Again, when you acknowledge the other person both verbally and nonverbally, you build trust and increase rapport. And you'll probably learn something, too!

7. Abstain from judging. As someone once advised, "Grow antennae, not horns." If you prejudge someone as shallow or crazy or ill-informed, you automatically cease paying attention to what they say. Therefore, a basic rule of listening is to judge only after you've heard and evaluated what they have said. Don't jump to conclusions based on how they look, what you've heard about them, or how nervous they are.

    In fact, a good exercise would be to go out of your way to listen to a difficult speaker—maybe someone with a thick accent, someone who talks much more rapidly or slowly than you, or someone who uses a lot of big words. Whatever difficulty this speaker poses, seize it as an opportunity not to prejudge but to practice your listening skills. Given some time, you'll become more comfortable and effective in listening to diverse styles.

8. Listen with empathy. No matter how outrageous, inconsiderate, false, self-centered, or pompous the person you're talking to seems, remember, he or she is simply trying to survive, just like you. We're all participating in the

same physical and person deserves more pity than scorn. "The wounded deer leaps highest," Emily Dickinson wrote, and it's true.

Listening with empathy means asking yourself, Where is this person's anger coming from? What is he or she asking for? What can I do that's reasonable and not condemning? You're not everyone's shrink, and you don't have to carry the weight of the world on your back; but, on the other hand, if you can think through what makes this person behave like this, perhaps you'll be inclined to cut them a little slack. Genuinely listening well is, at its heart, an act of love, and as such, may help heal.

9. Be sensitive to emotional deaf spots. Deaf spots are words that make your mind wander or go off on a mental tangent. They automatically produce a mental barrier that impedes listening. Everybody is affected that way by certain words.

    For example, a speaker giving a talk to savings-and-loan personnel kept saying "bank." To members of that industry, banks and S&Ls are very different things, and so each reference to them as "bankers" irritated the audience and aroused emotions that temporarily derailed their listening.

    So be alert to what your own deaf spots are and make adjustments. Also, try to find out what raises the hackles of other people, then avoid those words so as to raise the likely level of listening.

10. Create and use an active-listening attitude. Learning to be an active listener is like learning to be an active jogger. It takes effort. You start little by little and work upward. It's as much a state of mind as a physical activity. Besides, as you work longer and get better, it pays ever-increasing dividends.

    An active-listening attitude can help tremendously in breaking your poor listening habits. Exercising such an attitude means—

    • Appreciating that listening is as powerful as speech. What someone says to you is just as critical as what you have to say to them.

    • Realizing that listening saves time and effort. Those who listen make fewer mistakes, cause fewer misunderstandings, and make fewer false starts.

    • Understanding that listening to everybody is important and worthwhile. Look for that something you can learn from each and every person you meet. This will gratify some people and astonish the rest.

Dr. Tony Alessandra has authored 13 books, recorded over 50 audio and video programs, and delivered over 2,000 keynote speeches since 1976. This article has been adapted from Dr. Alessandra's book *Communicating at Work*. If you would like more information about Dr. Alessandra's books, audio tape sets, and video programs, or if you would like to contact Dr. Alessandra about a speaking engagement, call his office at 1-800-222-4383 or visit his website at http://www.alessandra.com

Authors Note: CARESS relates to the following:

☐ **Concentrate.** Focus your attention on the speaker and only on the speaker.

☐ **Acknowledge.** Acknowledge your speaker by demonstrating your interest and attention.

☐ **Research.** Gather information about your speaker through the skillful use of questions and statements.

☐ **Emotional Control.** Exercise emotional control by dealing with highly-charged messages in a thoughtful manner. This leads to early problem solving.

☐ **Sensing.** Sense the nonverbal messages of your speaker by observing what he's saying with his body language.

☐ **Structure.** Structure or organize the information you get through your listening, observation, and note-taking.

Appendix E
Communication Skills
Self-Assessment Exercise

The following self-assessment exercise is designed to help you evaluate your own interpersonal communication skills and style and to provide you with helpful tips for becoming a good communicator and team player.

For each of the following, pick the option that best describes your communication style. (24 total)

1. ___ A. When conversing with others, I usually do most of the talking.

   ___ B. When conversing with others, I usually let the other person do most of the talking.

   C. When conversing with others, I try to equalize my participation in the conversation.

   Best answer: C. Conversations should be a balanced two-way flow of dialogue.

2. ___ A. When I first meet someone, I wait for the other person to make the introduction first.

   ___ B. When I first meet someone, I introduce myself with a smile and offer a handshake.

   ___ C. When I first meet someone, I hug the person.

Best answer: B. It's good to initiate the introduction and introduce yourself with a handshake and smile. If shaking hands is difficult, a quick head nod is a good substitute. Initiating the introduction with a smile and handshake (or head nod) helps build rapport.

3.   ___ A. I usually "warm-up" new conversations with small talk.

   ___ B. I usually avoid small talk and jump into more important matters.

   ___ C. I usually avoid starting conversations.

Best answer: A. It's good to initiate conversations with small talk. Topics to warm up the conversation might include the weather, news of interest, or impressions about the current activity (if you're at a meeting, staff party, or other gathering, for example).

Examples of conversation starters:

> "It's sure warm today, isn't it?"
> "Did you hear about the big accident on the freeway? Traffic's backed up for miles."
> "What did you think about the Blazers game last night?"
> "This is a nice party, isn't it?"
> "Could I get you something to drink?"

4.   ___ A. I make an effort to remember and use peoples' names.

   ___ B. I don't pay attention to names, as I tend to forget them.

   ___ C. I only learn the names of important people.

Best answer: A. It's good to call people by name whenever possible. It makes a good, lasting impression, and it makes the other person feel important and special. To help remember names, try these techniques:

Repetition: After the person tells you his or her name, immediately use it several times in the conversation.

> "It's nice to meet you, Bob."
> "I agree with you, Bob."
> "That was a great joke, Bob!"

Association: Associate the person's name to something unique and special. You might:

Associate the person's name with a unique feature about the person. For example:

"Gilda has beautiful green eyes."
Think "GG": Green Gilda
"Jack tells funny jokes."
Think "JJ": Joking Jack

Associate the name with a visual picture. For example:

"Sandy"—visualize a sandy beach.
"Glenn"—visualize John Glenn launching into space.

Associate the name with a personal connection. For example:

"Brian"—My uncle's name is Brian.
"Lucy"—I had a turtle named Lucy.

Jot: Jot the person's name down with an identifying description that will help jog your memory later. For example:

"Chuck"—tall, glasses, works in Accounting, has twin sister, runs marathons, new to Portland.

5. ___ A. I frequently use courtesy words and phrases: "Please," "Thank you," "You're welcome," "I'm sorry."

___ B. I occasionally use courtesy words and phrases.

___ C. I never use courtesy words and phrases.

Best answer: A. Regular use of courtesy words and phrases is important to show politeness and build rapport.

6. ___ A. I tend to be serious and don't smile often while conversing.

___ B. I smile all the time while conversing.

___ C. I smile at appropriate times while conversing.

Best answer: C. Smiling when greeting people and at appropriate times greatly helps build rapport.

7. ___ A. I make eye contact while conversing.

___ B. I sometimes make eye contact while conversing.

_____ C. I never make eye contact while conversing.

Best answer: A. Making eye contact is important for building rapport. It gives the impression that you're interested and engaged in the conversation and that you have self-confidence.

Eye contact should include frequent breaks to avoid staring (which can make the other person uncomfortable). Break eye contact frequently—glance down to the side, then quickly make eye contact again. Glancing down to the side is important. If you glance to the side (as if looking out the window, for example) or look up, it gives the person the impression that you're distracted and not paying attention to what's being said. This quickly breaks down rapport.

8.   _____ A. While conversing, I hold my head still at all times.

       _____ B. While conversing, I nod my head at appropriate times.

       _____ C. While conversing, I nod my head constantly.

Best answer: B. Occasionally nodding your head to indicate you agree or understand helps build rapport. Again, it shows you are interested and engaged in the conversation.

9.   _____ A. While conversing, I stand one foot away from the person.

       _____ B. While conversing, I stand two to three feet away from the person.

       _____ C. While conversing, I stand five to six feet away from the person.

Best answer: B. Your arm's length is the appropriate distance (between two to three feet). Standing closer than arm-length makes the other person feel uncomfortable (or feel threatened). Standing farther away breaks down rapport.

10.   _____ A. I often stand while talking to a person who is sitting.

       _____ B. I often sit while talking to a person who is sitting.

       _____ C. I often lean down while talking to a person who is sitting.

Best answer: B. Communicating at eye level helps build rapport. So, if the person is sitting and a chair is available, take a seat! There's one exception: If you walk into your supervisor's office or co-worker's office, it's best to ask the supervisor or co-worker if you can sit down first. Even better, wait for an invitation to sit. The person may not have time to talk at that moment.

11. ___ A. To end a conversation, I often just leave.

___ B. To end a conversation, I begin to look impatient hoping the person will get the hint.

___ C. To end a conversation, I wrap up with a closing statement.

Best answer: C. It's best to bring the conversation to an end by making a polite closing comment or gesture. Good closing (wrap-up) comments:

"I've enjoyed talking with you."
"Let me give you my business card."
"Well, I need to go speak with...."
"Do you know a person I can contact?"

12. ___ A. If a co-worker has put on weight, I say nothing about it.

___ B. If a co-worker has put on weight, I tell the person that he or she has changed in appearance.

___ C. If a co-worker has put on weight, I honestly tell the person that he or she looks fat.

Best answer: A. It's best to say nothing. Never say anything that might hurt or offend the person. It's called being tactful. It's always best to give compliments; only say things that will make the person feel good:

"I like your dress."
"That's a nice shirt."

13. ___ A. When I'm listening to the speaker, I often cross my arms over my chest.

___ B. When I'm listening to the speaker, I often lean back and turn my body away from the speaker.

___ C. When I'm listening to the speaker, I often lean slightly forward and face my body toward the speaker.

Best answer: C. Leaning slightly forward and facing the speaker shows you're interested, and it helps build rapport. Sitting with your arms crossed over your chest gives the message that you are defensive. Leaning back or turning your body away from the speaker gives the message that you are bored, disinterested, or feel in charge. Such body language breaks down rapport.

14. ___ A. When I cross my leg, I cross my leg facing the speaker.

___ B. When I cross my leg, I cross my leg away from the speaker.

___ C. When I cross my leg, I bob my foot.

Best answer: A. Crossing your leg toward the speaker shows you're interested, and it builds rapport. Crossing your leg away from the speaker gives the message that you are defensive, disinterested, or feel in charge. In essence, you are putting up a subtle barrier. And if you bob or swing your foot, you're sending the message that you're anxious or nervous!

15. ___ A. While listening, I tend to be distracted by things going on around me.

___ B. While listening, I listen for meaning and ask questions.

___ C. While listening, I watch the person speak, but I don't "hear" a word.

Best answer: B. If you're a good listener, you keep mentally busy searching for for meaning in the message, and you ask questions. This mental "search for meaning" helps keep you focused, attentive, and engaged. If you get easily distracted, try taking notes if the setting is appropriate. Note-taking helps focus your attention, as you must mentally "search for meaning" and listen for information in order to take notes. This might be helpful in meetings, for example. If you watch someone speak but you don't "hear" a word, gauge if you are bored, are tired, have a gap between your speaking and listening rates, or are experiencing "emotional deafness." We all experience emotional deafness on occasion, especially when we're feeling overwhelmed, upset, or nervous. You know this is the case when you hear people ask, "I'm sorry, what did you say?" or make the comment—"I have a lot on my mind right now. Could you repeat what you said?" If it's a frequent problem, gauge the source and seek help if needed.

16. ___ A. When someone talks about an unfortunate or sad experience, I don't comment about it.

___ B. When someone talks about an unfortunate or sad experience, I try to change the subject.

___ C. When someone talks about an unfortunate or sad experience, I try to relate to the person's feelings and show sensitivity to his or her misfortune.

Best answer: C. Empathizing with another person's feelings helps build rapport. It's called "reaching out to people." Empathy can be shown by making comments such as—

"That must have been a scary (or upsetting) experience for you."
"I felt the same way when that happened to me."
"I know (understand) how you feel."
"I can imagine how you feel."
"I would feel that way too in your situation."

17. ___ A. When I discuss a topic, I tend to talk about and focus on positive aspects.

___ B. When I discuss a topic, I tend to talk about and focus on the negative aspects.

___ C. When I discuss a topic, I tend to complain.

Best answer: A. Focusing on the positive aspects draws people's attention in a favorable way, and people enjoy the conversation more. People are generally more attracted to a person who has a "positive outlook on life." And when it comes to work evaluations, positive-minded people generally do better. Consider the following examples:

Positive:	"The plan has some good ideas."
Negative:	"The plan has some serious problems."
Complaint:	"No one ever listens to my ideas."

Positive:	"These changes might have some benefits."
Negative:	"These changes would be awful."
Complaint:	"I'm always having to relearn and re-do everything around here."

18. ___ A. When I have a negative opinion or comment, I just say it.

___ B. When I have a negative opinion or comment, I lead in with a positive comment first.

___ C. When I have a negative opinion or comment, I say nothing.

Best answer: B. It's best to say something positive first, then express a negative opinion or comment in a tactful way. Consider these examples:

Positive lead:

> "I like many aspects of your idea (positive lead), but it may not work well for this department." (tactfully stated)

> Interpretation: The idea won't work.

Positive lead:

> "You did a nice job setting the bread plates and glasses (positive lead), but the forks need to be placed to the left." (tactfully stated)

> Interpretation: The forks are in the wrong place.

Positive lead (with empathy):

> "I know you worked a long time on this (positive lead), but it would look better retyped." (tactfully stated)

> Interpretation: It needs to be retyped.

19. ___ A. When I receive unfavorable feedback, I note where I need to improve.

  ___ B. When I receive unfavorable feedback, I get angry and defensive.

  ___ C. When I receive unfavorable feedback, I deny the problem, make excuses, or plead ignorance.

Best answer: A. When you receive feedback, it's important to know what you do well, but it's equally important to know where improvements can be made to increase your chances for success. Few people do everything well, and you've undoubtedly heard the saying "No one is perfect." Simply make note of "weak" areas (we all have them!) and make the necessary changes. Honest feedback is truly a gift. It usually means someone cares and wishes to see you succeed.

20. ___ A. When I give a person negative feedback, I focus on the person's observable work or behavior and offer suggestions.

  ___ B. When I give a person negative feedback, I focus on what I don't like about the person.

___ C. When I give a person negative feedback, I simply tell the person what to do right.

Best answer: A. When you give negative feedback, you should focus on and communicate your observations of the person's work or behavior, not focus on or judge the person. Focus on performance, not personality. After sharing your observation about the person's work or behavior, offer suggestions in a tactful way. Consider these examples:

Example 1:

> "The forms you completed were thoroughly done (positive lead), but I noticed (observation) there were a few spelling errors (work feedback). Perhaps you should turn on the spell checker in Word (suggestion)."
>
>> Important: Notice how it says, "There are a few spelling errors" instead of You made a few spelling errors." Leave out "you" whenever possible.

Example 2:

> "Your presentation covered the main points very well (positive lead), but I noticed (observation) contact information was left out (work feedback). I wonder if it might be good to include a contact name and phone number (suggestion)."

Example 3:

> "I like your ideas (positive lead), but it appears (observation) the delivery (communication style or behavior) weakens them. Perhaps they could be written down and handed out for everyone to review (suggestion).

21. ___ A. When I give a person negative feedback, I do it around others so everyone can hear.

___ B. When I give a person negative feedback, I do it in front of the supervisor.

___ C. When I give a person negative feedback, I talk with the person alone in a private place.

Best answer: C. It's always best to meet the person privately and away from other people so others can't hear.

22.   ___ A. When I disagree with a person, I listen first, ask questions for clarification, then disagree non-judgmentally.

___ B. When I disagree with a person, I quickly point out the person is wrong and why.

___ C. When I disagree with a person, I say little or nothing.

Best answer: A. It's fine to disagree, but it's important to disagree agreeably. This means you should—

1) show respect for the other person's ideas,
2) listen attentively until the person is done,
3) ask questions if needed,
4) disagree non-judgmentally, and, if possible,
5) offer an alternative solution.

Consider these examples:

"I respect your view, John, (shows respect) but I think the problem is due to a lack of time (point of disagreement). One way to solve the problem might be to computerize repair reports (offered solution)."

"I hear what you're saying (shows respect), but it seems the staff would do better, not worse, with flextime schedules (point of disagreement). I would suggest we try it for six months (offered solution)."

23.   ___ A. When I'm in a group, I tend to frown a lot.

___ B. When I'm in a group, I tend to smile and use humor at appropriate times.

___ C. When I'm in a group, I tend to be serious.

Best answer: B. At appropriate times, it's always good to smile. When used at appropriate times and in appropriate ways, humor is beneficial to group dynamics. Humor helps "break the ice" when people first meet. Humor helps relieve stress and tension. A humorous observation and comment helps lower the heat when a heated discussion gets too "hot." And most importantly, humor helps build team cohesiveness.

If you observe people at a gathering, you'll notice people naturally gravitate toward people considered "approachable." Approachable people are the ones who smile, they are the ones who add humor and lightness to conversations, and they are the ones who make fun of themselves in a lighthearted and humorous way. In any group setting, smiles attract, and humor bonds people together. Do you know a good joke?

Idea: If you're like many people who have difficulty remembering humorous lines, puns, anecdotal stories, or jokes, consider creating a humor file. Clip and save humorous jokes, stories, and puns from the newspaper. Write down and save jokes and funny stories you hear. Your file will be a good resource to draw upon for upcoming social events and gatherings.

This last item has four choices. Which one best describes you?

24. ___ A. I'm a "hands-on" person. I tend to—

- prefer hands-on experiences and activities
- focus on tasks to be done
- refrain from discussions
- think in a logical and organized way
- do things in an orderly way
- have difficulty adjusting to change

___ B. I'm a "thinker." I tend to—

- enjoy listening to a logical presentation of ideas
- enjoy analyzing problems and finding systematic ways to solve problems
- enjoy creating models based on theory and information
- like structure and organization
- act slowly in making decisions
- show more interest in ideas than people

___ C. I'm an "explorer." I tend to—

- try things by trial and error
- explore practical uses for ideas and theories
- make decisions that provide quick solutions

- decide quickly

- take risks

- enjoy change

- rely more on people than books for information

___ D. I'm a "free thinker." I tend to—

- base views and opinions on feelings

- enjoy tossing around ideas (brainstorming)

- approach and view problems and experiences from different perspectives

- rely on intuition, not logic, when making decisions

- dislike structure

Best answer: The one that fits you! The four choices above describe and identify four communication (and learning) styles, and no one style is better than the others. This part of the exercise merely serves to illustrate how people think, act, learn, and communicate differently. Each person in a group may have a different style.

How well you are able to recognize, respect, and adjust to other people's ways of communicating and "doing things" is a key to success when working with a supervisor, a group of people, or a class instructor.

For example, if you are a "free thinker," you like to brainstorm ideas and do what "feels right." You might find it frustrating to work with (or learn from a "thinker," a person who focuses on and approaches tasks and ideas based on logic, reasoning, and organized structure. The "thinker" would be equally frustrated working with a person or group that loosely brainstorms ideas all afternoon. How successfully "opposites" work together largely depends on how well each person adjusts to the others' styles. Flexibility and compromise are the keys.

If you find yourself working with a supervisor, co-worker, team player, or instructor who has a style that differs from your own, recognize and respect the other person's style and learn to accommodate it as much as possible.

Consider these "how-to" tips:

How to accommodate a "hands-on" style

- Arrive promptly.
- Pay very close attention to deadlines.
- Don't procrastinate or make excuses.
- Be organized.
- Accept structure.
- Try to do things in an exact and precise way.
- Make brief and "to-the-point" comments—don't ramble.
- Minimize discussion—get to the task.
- Ask questions in a brief, concise way.
- Use concrete terms and explanations (not abstract).
- Do things in sequential and orderly steps.
- Discuss and show practical applications.
- Demonstrate to illustrate an idea or point.
- Allow for "hands-on" project-type tasks.

How to accommodate a "thinker" style

- Arrive promptly.
- Pay very close attention to deadlines.
- Don't procrastinate or make excuses.
- Be organized.
- Use outlines, charts, graphs, and spatial mapping to show information and the relationship of ideas.
- Provide data.
- Provide documentation.
- Be open to the use of abstract explanations and terms.

- Support information with facts (proof).
- Support views and opinions with logic and evidence.
- Focus on main ideas, related details, and logical conclusions.
- Be open to topics that allow for debate.
- Be patient with quick and sudden moves from idea to idea.
- Allow for research-type tasks.

How to accommodate an "explorer" style

- Be open to new ideas.
- Be open to change.
- Allow room for creative innovation.
- Be open-minded to opinions and views.
- Be attentive.
- Show interest.
- Relate ideas to the real world, using real-world examples.
- Focus on processes and applications rather than facts.
- Be willing to take a risk or investigate.
- Be patient with disorganization.
- Share humor and laugh at jokes.
- Be patient with jumps from one idea to another.
- Be willing to discuss ideas.
- Allow for innovative and creative tasks.

How to accommodate a "free thinker" style

- Smile and be friendly.
- Be willing to chat and visit.
- Share personal experiences.
- Participate in discussions and activities.

- Lean forward—be attentive and show interest.
- Use gestures and positive body language.
- Use humor.
- Be sincere.
- Use images, pictures, and color.
- Apply personal meaning to ideas.
- Show how ideas and details apply to life.
- Show interest and concern for people.
- Be patient if describes extensively.
- Avoid questioning or challenging the person's insight or logic.
- Be patient with interruptions.
- Be open to use of metaphoric language and expression.
- Don't force structure—allow room for flexibility.
- Allow for interactive tasks.

Prepared by Robin Jacobs, Office for Students with Disabilities, Portland Community College, Portland, OR. Used With Permission.

Appendix F
Take-Action Form

Staff Meeting

Date: _____ Place: _____

Names of Participants:

_____   _____

_____   _____

_____   _____

_____   _____

_____   _____

Agenda Item	Decision Reached	Follow-Up Activity	Responsibility	Deadline
1.				
2.				
3.				
4.				

Agenda Item	Decision Reached	Follow-Up Activity	Responsibility	Deadline
5.				
6.				
7.				
8.				
9.				
10.				

Appendix G
Record of Counseling Form

RECORD OF COUNSELING			
ADMINISTRATIVE DATA			
Name (Last, First, MI)	Title	Location of Counseling	Date of Counseling
Organization		Name and Title of Counselor	
BACKGROUND INFORMATION			
Purpose of Counseling (Leader states the reason for the counseling, e.g. Performance/Professional or Event-Oriented counseling, and includes the leader's facts and observations prior to the counseling):			
SUMMARY OF COUNSELING **Complete this section during or immediately after counseling.**			
Key Points of Discussion:			

Plan of Action (Outlines actions that the subordinate will perform after the counseling session to reach the agreed-upon goal(s). The actions must be specific enough to modify or maintain the subordinate's behavior and include a specific timeline for implementation and assessment (Part IV below):

Session Closing (The leader summarizes the key points of the session and ensures the subordinate understands the plan of action. The subordinate agrees/disagrees and provides remarks if appropriate):

Individual counseled: I agree / disagree with the information above

 Individual counseled remarks:

Signature of Individual Counseled: .... Date: ....

Leader's Responsibilities (Leader's responsibilities in implementing the plan of action):

Signature of Counselor: .... Date: ....

ASSESSMENT OF THE PLAN OF ACTION

Assessment (Did the plan of action achieve the desired results? This section is completed by both the leader and the individual counseled and provides useful information for follow-up counseling):

Counselor: .... Individual Counseled:......................... Date of Assessment: ....

Appendix H
Creating an Organizational Vision

When you begin the process of strategic planning, visioning comes first. When visioning the change, ask yourself, "What is our preferred future?" and be sure to:

- Draw on the beliefs, mission, and environment of the organization.

- Describe what you want to see in the future.

- Be specific to each organization.

- Be positive and inspiring.

- Do not assume that the organization will have the same framework as it does today.

- Be open to dramatic modifications to current organization, methodology, teaching techniques, facilities, etc.

Key Components for Your Vision

<u>Incorporate Your Beliefs</u>
Your vision must be encompassed by your beliefs.

- Your beliefs must meet your organizational goals as well as community goals.

- Your beliefs are a statement of your values.

- Your beliefs are a public/visible declaration of your expected outcomes.

- Your beliefs must be precise and practical.

- Your beliefs will guide the actions of all involved.

- Your beliefs reflect the knowledge, philosophy, and actions of all.

- Your beliefs are a key component of strategic planning.

Create a Mission Statement

Once you have clarified your beliefs, build on them to define your mission statement which is a statement of purpose and function.

- Your mission statement draws on your belief statements.

- Your mission statement must be future oriented and portray your organization as it will be, as if it already exists.

- Your mission statement must focus on one common purpose.

- Your mission statement must be specific to the organization, not generic.

- Your mission statement must be a short statement, not more than one or two sentences.

Benefits of Visioning

The process and outcomes of visioning may seem vague and superfluous. The long-term benefits are substantial, however. Visioning:

- Breaks you out of boundary thinking.

- Provides continuity and avoids the stutter effect of planning fits and starts.

- Identifies direction and purpose.

- Alerts stakeholders to needed change.

- Promotes interest and commitment.

- Promotes laser-like focus.

- Encourages openness to unique and creative solutions.

- Encourages and builds confidence.

- Builds loyalty through involvement (ownership).

- Results in efficiency and productivity.

Vision Killers

As you engage in the visioning process, be alert to the following vision killers:

- Tradition
- Fear of ridicule
- Stereotypes of people, conditions, roles and governing councils
- Complacency of some stakeholders
- Fatigued leaders
- Short-term thinking
- "Naysayers"

Appendix I
Motivational Management: Developing Leadership Skills

by Diane M. Eade

Whether you work in a hospital, private practice, health-maintenance organization, government facility, or university, you probably supervise other people. Your behavior as a manager has a direct impact on staff performance, productivity, satisfaction, and turnover. In this article, an expert management consultant examines qualities of managers who motivate, providing proven techniques to inspire those who work for you.

Perhaps the single most important technique for motivating the people you supervise is to treat them the same way you wish to be treated: as responsible professionals. It sounds simple; just strike the right balance of respect, dignity, fairness, incentive, and guidance, and you will create a motivated, productive, satisfying, and secure work environment.

Unfortunately, as soon as the complexities of our evolving healthcare delivery system mix with human relationships, even the best-intentioned supervisors can find the management side of their jobs deteriorating into chaos. Today's healthcare providers face expanding workloads, fewer resources, greater patient expectations, increasing threats (e.g., malpractice lawsuits), and closer scrutiny, especially from third-party providers. The art of healing is being transformed into a business. And like it or not, nurse practitioners and physician assistants often find themselves in middle-management roles, with tremendous responsibility and little real authority. Job performance is reflected more in the bottom line than in the quality of patient care. Why, in this environment, do some managers thrive while others burn out? The answers lie in each manager's ability to inspire trust, loyalty, commitment, and collegiality among team members. The same techniques that work elsewhere in business can bring success in nursing and medicine—whether you're working in clinical practice, administration, or academia. More often than not, though, the task can be accomplished only by replacing learned behaviors with newer, more effective models.

Unlearning Autocratic Styles

Good management technique used to be simple. The boss told employees what to do, and they complied. No one worried if somebody's feelings were hurt along the way. Employees who failed to toe the line were either whipped into shape or fired. These authoritarian managers believed that authority should (in a moral sense) be obeyed. Therefore, they expected unquestioning obedience from their subordinates and they, in turn, submissively obeyed their own superiors. What could be simpler? Fear ran the work setting. The system was efficient.

Healthcare delivery, in particular, followed this autocratic model. The physician's order ruled, without question or negotiation. Physicians, in turn, had their own hierarchy. Authority was understood, respected, and obeyed.

The example set by past generations has led to huge numbers of autocratic managers today. Some lead this way because they honestly and consciously believe it is the best management style. For most, however, they are merely imitating how they were treated throughout their careers (particularly at a first job). The cycle works very much like child abuse, where the abused child grows up to be an abusive adult. If you were managed by an autocrat, it is very likely that your most natural, comfortable method of management will reflect that of a previous supervisor, especially your first.

Physician assistants and NPs find themselves particularly vulnerable to this cycle of abuse. Both professions faced great hostility from the moment of their inception. Today's NP or PA leaders spent years struggling to prove their professions' full worth, overcoming the mentality that nonphysician providers were hired to answer telephones and empty bedpans. Frighteningly, today's senior PAs and NPs are the product of that mentality.

Why Change?

While fear as a management style can achieve impressive short-term results, the long-term consequences can be devastating. With demand high and supply short for NPs and PAs, no manager can afford to alienate other clinicians. Similarly, efficient support staff are also becoming harder to recruit and train, as the technology of the workplace speeds along at a blinding pace. Disgruntled employees may vent their frustrations by being rude to patients, performing poorly, quitting, or complaining to upper management; some supervisors may even face lawsuits for treating subordinates unfairly.

An autocratic management style results in high staff turnover and low employee morale. Low morale, in turn, causes a decline in productivity and in the quality of service provided to your patients. And while many autocratic managers still populate the American healthcare system, reform demanding higher efficiency and productivity will eventually squeeze such managers out of the marketplace. In short, motivational management produces better results; those who focus on positive reinforcement rather than fear and intimidation will be the successful managers in the next millennium.

Understanding Change

Because autocratic management is a learned behavior focusing on dramatic, short-term results, true change can come only from within. Such change requires an understanding of the need for a new management approach. Motivating yourself to change is the first step in learning to motivate others.

Decisions that incorporate the ideas of a group of people are vastly superior to the single viewpoint of one person imposed on the rest of the group.

Rapid, relentless advances in technology and vast amounts of new information pounding at us every day make it impossible for a single leader to know more than the sum of his or her subordinates. Each team member's knowledge and perspective are essential to good decision-making. Decisions that incorporate the ideas of a group of people are vastly superior to the single viewpoint of one person imposed on the rest of the group.

In past generations, employees stayed with a company for the duration of an entire career. Today, people change jobs several times during their working years, and many change careers altogether. This adaptation to change gives employees more options. When a well-trained employee quits, the business incurs not only out-of-pocket hiring and training costs, but the "opportunity cost" of having a less effective, brand-new employee who will require three to six months of training before becoming a productive, efficient member of the team.

Fundamental changes in American society also herald the end of the autocratic manager. The extended family unit—two-parent households supported by closely-linked (geographically) grandparents, aunts, uncles, siblings, and cousins—is the exception, not the rule. Divorce and geographic mobility undermine the role of the nuclear family. Most managers accept how child care, family leave, and single-parent households are changing the workplace. But what about the void that now exists where there was once a powerful family unit of "belonging"?

The role of the traditional family is being replaced by the workplace. More and more, employees look for jobs where people matter. Such employees want to work with managers, not for them. This presents a huge challenge for businesses and creates a responsibility for which most managers are unprepared.

Breaking Established Patterns

Autocratic management requires less skill and effort than participatory management, so the decision to change requires true commitment. In the autocratic model, you simply exercise your authority, make a decision, and take responsibility for the results. Participatory management means learning and playing by a whole new set of rules. Such change is never easy.

The first step toward a new style of leadership is deciding that you need and want to change. Involving your staff in decision-making requires diverse and refined interpersonal skills. You need to learn the capabilities and aspirations of each subordinate in order to execute participative techniques without wasting vast amounts of time. Time constraints, personality traits, and lack of consistent motivation often combine to work against managers' efforts to develop these skills. Behavioral change takes time, focus, and practice.

Pathway to Success

Good management, like good health, is the result of daily conditioning. What qualities lead to successful motivational management? The following strategies—plan; teach; delegate, not dump; encourage independent thinking; build a team; listen; set an example; accept responsibility; and share the spotlight—are proven in becoming an effective leader in today's business world.

Plan

Planning may be the most important and most overlooked aspect of effective management. Take, for example, a practice in which clinicians are expected to see thirty patients each day, or a hospital where each practitioner routinely manages twenty critically-ill patients. To that, add walk-ins and emergencies. Triage is random, with little thought given to support and backup. The clinician loses all control of time, constantly running from one crisis to another.

Consider, too, the clinician who routinely directs clerical staff to begin work on numerous projects, without establishing priorities or understanding the amount of work involved. Many of the projects are never completed; others are rushed and sloppy. A pattern of "false starts" develops, leaving employees feeling disempowered and frustrated.

Good planning involves a sense of strategic direction. What does the team need to do, in a global sense, to get to an established goal? What constraints can be identified, and can each member of the team contribute?

It must be noted that solid strategies are necessary, but not sufficient in and of themselves, for good planning. Detailed action plans based on those strategies are critical. The key to effective management is how you involve your subordinates in the development of these action plans. Solicit input from all and listen with an open mind. The people who actually do the work can provide you with invaluable insight into how to get the job done. Negotiate a consensus, and then make certain everyone agrees on who will do what, by when. Once an action plan is adopted, make sure the team has the resources (e.g., funds, equipment, and human power) to execute those plans.

Become a Teacher

A role model for the effective participatory supervisor is the teacher who views any shortcoming as an opportunity for you to grow, someone who always focuses on your potential when he or she works with you. Such managers consistently support their employees, helping them discover the paths to success.

To help yourself reach your potential as a participatory manager, try some of these techniques:

First, list the benefits of becoming a good teacher for your subordinates, and share that list with the people you supervise. There's nothing like a public commitment to keep your own motivation high!

Next, approach teaching as a reflection of your personal values. Know that your personal power is greatly enhanced when you live up to your own principles and values.

Remember that to be an effective teacher you do not need to know everything your subordinates know. Rather, you must invest your energy in creating opportunities for your subordinates to become experts in their skill areas. Then, give them the chance to demonstrate their expertise.

View teaching as your primary responsibility. It is not an extracurricular activity for effective managers. And as your subordinates grow, reward them; nurture their careers and professional growth in every way possible.

Delegate, Never Dump
The easiest way to become good at delegation is to surround yourself with subordinates whose abilities you respect; then you would be foolish not to use them to the best of their capabilities. When people sense that you expect great things from them, they tend to be challenged by that expectation and work hard to live up to it. Load your people with responsibility, provide them with the resources to do the job, and never be punitive when they make mistakes.

Delegation crosses the line and becomes dumping when we delegate only the work we don't want to do ourselves; keep all the "glorious" fun projects for ourselves; fail to provide adequate resources for our subordinates to complete their work; delegate all the responsibility and none of the authority for the job; or abandon our subordinates, failing to provide them with timing requirements, project guidelines, or our personal counsel when they need it.

Encourage Independent Thinking
Consistently encourage your subordinates to come to you with problems and solutions. If they come to you only with the problem, it's your job to elicit their opinion for correcting the situation. Listen to their suggestions; draw them out. Help them to think the solution through. Ask them a series of questions that encourage them and lead them to a workable solution.

Such independent thinking demands your recognition that your solution to a problem is not the only solution; it may not even be the best solution. Give your subordinates the latitude to try new options, within reasonable limits, and your workers will start to develop their real potential.

Build a Team
Similar to the teacher analogy, effective participatory managers strive to build cohesive teams, seeing themselves as the team's captain. The team captain inspires excellence and earns loyalty, serving as a role model to be admired, not feared.

The most effective teams comprise members with diverse skills and personalities. These are also the most difficult teams to manage. It can be frustrating work, but the rewards are tremendous when you watch the team become greater than the sum of its parts.

In planning, you determined the goals of the team. To manage the team successfully, make sure everyone clearly understands his or her role in reaching those goals. Communicate the rules or norms for operating together. For instance, a rule that many successful teams adopt is, "When you have a problem with any team member, it is your responsibility to discuss the problem directly with that team member. If you approach another team member instead, you will immediately be referred to the team member who has caused you difficulty."

As the team leader, it also becomes your responsibility to help integrate the individual personalities of team members. Encourage cooperation and coordination among members. This may occasionally mean sharing the perspective of one member with another to facilitate mutual understanding and respect.

Listen

Many managers talk about being good listeners, yet this skill often remains an area where they could improve substantially. The benefits of good listening are numerous. Relationships improve, productivity and work performance are enhanced, team spirit is fostered, morale increases, and your staff gains better perspective and understanding of your mission. Good listening skills engender trust, and trust is what separates effective participatory leaders from autocratic managers.

If you're listening effectively, the odds are that your subordinate is talking 80% of the time, and you're talking only 20% of the time. When you speak, you ask short, simple questions that draw the person out. What's more, you ask questions in a concerned, nonthreatening style and tone. Good listeners let their subordinates vent when necessary and acknowledge their feelings.

It is critical that the listener stay open and nondefensive, conveying genuine concern, no matter what the staff member says. Maintain the attitude that this person is your teammate and wants to improve things. Learn all you possibly can from your teammates so you are able to address their concerns effectively. Demonstrating your concern by helping team members resolve problems to their satisfaction not only strengthens the unit, it also provides flexibility for you when problems that are beyond your control arise. Past successes build trust, so your teammates are much more likely to listen to you and be reasonable when a problem exceeds your authority.

Set an Example

People rarely learn from what we tell them to do. More often they learn from example. If you have any doubts, go back to the discussion of autocratic managers and child abusers. Not only does the example you set dictate your success as a manager, but it teaches tomorrow's clinicians how to lead. So set a good example.

Start by living up to the rules you've already negotiated with team members. Treat each staff person with respect. Be kind and courteous. Keep your cool in crisis situations. Your calm will be just as contagious as your panic and temper flare-ups. Keep your word—to the letter. Nothing undermines trust in a professional setting more precipitously than a manager who breaks his or her commitments.

Accept Responsibility
Perhaps the most frightening aspect of management is that you've become responsible for someone else's performance. People do things their own way, and sometimes they make mistakes. While your subordinates are responsible to you for their mistakes, you are responsible to your manager for those mistakes. Don't pass the blame down to your subordinates. It's your department; the buck stops with you. Your team respects your integrity and trusts you to lead. You become a champion, not an oppressor.

Share the Spotlight
The flipside of accepting responsibility for everything that goes wrong is giving subordinates just credit for everything that goes right. Never take credit for a subordinate's work, and mention names at every possible opportunity.

Don't be afraid that this approach endangers your own career. You were made a supervisor because others in authority recognized your capabilities. The test of your value as a supervisor is your ability to create a productive, efficient team. Show management that working for you is the best thing that ever happened to your staff by drawing attention to each subordinate's excellent performance. If your team is performing at a high level, you won't need to blow your own horn—your value will be obvious.

What Will It Take to Be Successful?

- Assume responsibility for your own actions. If you are not successful, don't blame anyone else. Take it on the chin and learn from it.

- Assume responsibility for your emotional reactions. It's not what happens to you that matters; it's what it means to you that determines your reaction. Stand back and get perspective. Ask yourself, "What can we learn from this?" and it will be easier to control yourself.

- Identify the potential in each of your subordinates. Remember that people tend to live up to our expectations of them. Let your people know how terrific you think they are.

- Make an inventory of the resources at your disposal and use those resources to help your staff perform better. We live in a world of limited resources. Given that restraint, how can you optimize the results your department delivers?

- Be optimistic. Optimism is contagious, and so is pessimism. If your team is going to develop a positive, can-do attitude, you will need to set the tone.

- Develop a team vision for your department. Define what the team will become—make it inspiring! This is particularly powerful when you develop your vision as a team.

- Set specific and measurable goals to make that vision come true. Include time frames and resource requirements.

- Treat others with empathy and respect, no matter what. Gain the independence, power, and self-respect that come from doing the right thing, without regard to what others do.

- Think less about your own needs and more about the needs of your team. You will reap what you sow.

- Set an example—be a high performer. Work hard and intelligently. People will follow your example. Be honest with yourself and your team. Realize that, eventually, people who work with you will know you for who you are. Be open to their criticism and learn from it.

- Set a schedule for your own training and development—stick to it. Keep yourself growing and motivated. You're worth it.

- Model your management style after someone who inspires you. It's hard work to cut a path through the woods. It's much simpler to walk in someone else's tracks.

- Good input = good output. Find and consistently use good sources of management guidance for reading, viewing, and listening.

—Diane Eade, "Motivational Management: Developing Leadership Skills," *Clinician Reviews* 6, no. 10 (1996):115–125. Reprinted with permission.

0-595-31042-7